9 things successful people do differently

9 things successful people do differently

HEIDI GRANT
HALVORSON

Harvard Business Review Press
Boston, Massachusetts

The web addresses referenced in this book were live
and correct at the time of the book's publication but
may be subject to change.

ISBN: 978-1-4221-9340-2
LCCN: 2012036065

The paper used in this publication meets the re-
quirements of the American National Standard for
Permanence of Paper for Publications and Documents
in Libraries and Archives Z39.48-1992.

Contents

Introduction

Why have you been so successful in reaching *some* of your goals, but not others? If you aren't sure, you are far from alone in your confusion. It turns out that even very brilliant, highly accomplished people are pretty lousy when it comes to understanding why they succeed or fail. The intuitive answer—that you are born predisposed to certain talents and lacking in others—is really just one small piece of the puzzle. In fact, decades of research on achievement suggest that successful people reach their personal and professional goals not simply because of who they *are*, but more often because of what they *do*.

These are the nine things that successful people do—the strategies they use to set and pursue goals (sometimes without consciously realizing it) that, according to decades of research, have the biggest impact on performance. Scientific psychologists who study motivation, like myself, have conducted thousands of studies to identify and test the effectiveness (and limits) of these strategies. The good news is that the strategies are remarkably straightforward and easy to use. Reading this book, you will have lots of "Of course!" moments. Also some "Oh, I see, that makes sense," and a few "Wow, I had no idea" ones, too. In the end, not only will you have gained some insight into all the things you have been doing right all along, but you'll be able to identify the mistakes that have derailed you. More importantly, you'll be able to *use* that knowledge to your advantage from now on.

#1 Get Specific

When you set yourself a goal, try to be as specific as possible. "Lose five pounds" is a better goal than "lose some weight," because it gives you a clear idea of what success looks like. Knowing exactly what you want to achieve keeps you motivated until you get there. Also, think about the specific actions that you need to take to reach your goal. Just promising you'll "eat less" or "sleep more" is too vague; be clear and precise. "I'll be in bed by 10 p.m. on weeknights" leaves no room for doubt about what you need to do, and whether or not you've actually done it.

Whenever I ask people to tell me about their goals, I hear them say that they want to "get ahead at work" or "eat healthier" or "spend less and save more." To which I respond, "OK, but what will success *look like*? How will you know when you have reached your goal?" Usually, that's followed by a long pause, and a look of confusion. Then a reply something along the lines of "I hadn't really thought about that."

Taking the time to get specific and spell out *exactly* what you want to achieve removes the possibility of settling for less—of telling yourself that what you've done is "good enough." It also makes the course of action you need to take much clearer. (If my goal is to "get along better with my mother," it isn't obvious what I should do to reach it. But if I get more specific and instead make my goal to "speak to my mother at least twice a week," I know exactly what I need to do and how often I need to do it.) Thousands of studies have shown that getting specific is one of the most critical (though often overlooked) steps to take in reaching any goal.

Instead of "getting ahead at work," make your goal something more concrete, such as "a pay raise of at least $_____" or "a promotion to at least the _____ level." When what you are striving for is vague, it's too tempting to take the easy way out when you're feeling lazy, discouraged, or bored. But there's just no fooling yourself if you've set a specific goal; you know when you've reached it and when you haven't. If you haven't, you have little choice but to hang in there and keep trying if you want to succeed.

Being specific about what you want is just the first step. Next, you need to get specific about the obstacles that lie in the way of getting what you want. In fact, what you really need to do is go back and forth, thinking about the success you want to achieve *and* the steps it will take to get there. This strategy is called *mental contrasting*, and it is a remarkably effective way to set goals and strengthen your commitment.

To use the mental contrasting technique, first imagine how you will feel attaining your goal. Picture it as vividly as you can in your mind—really think about the details. Next, think about the obstacles that stand in your way. For instance, if you wanted to get a better, higher paying job, you would start by imagining the sense of pride and

excitement you would feel accepting a lu-
crative offer at a top firm. Then, you would
think about what stands between you and
that offer—namely, all the other really out-
standing candidates that will be applying
for the same job. Kind of makes you want to
polish up your résumé a bit, doesn't it?

That's called experiencing the *necessity
to act*; it's a state that is critical for reaching
your goal, because it gets the psychological
wheels in motion. Daydreaming about how
great it will be to land that job can be very
enjoyable, but it won't actually get you the
job. Mental contrasting turns wishes and
desires into reality by bringing attention
and clarity to what you will need to do to
make them happen.

In studies my colleagues and I have conducted—looking at situations ranging from

fifteen-year-olds doing summer prep for the PSAT, to human resource personnel trying to manage their time better, to singles trying to find a romantic partner, to pediatric nurses trying to improve communication with parents—the results are always the same. Mental contrasting reliably leads to greater effort, energy, planning, and overall higher rates of achieving goals. Taking a few moments to mentally go back and forth between the future you want and the hurdles you'll have to overcome to get there will help you find both the direction and motivation you need to succeed.

Putting It into Practice: Get Specific

1. Write down your goal.

> Example A: My goal is to get ahead at work.

Example B: My goal is to lose some weight.

2. Ask yourself, "How will I know when I have succeeded?" Describe the moment when you will *know* that you have reached your goal.

Example A: I will know I have gotten ahead when my boss tells me that I'm getting promoted to director.
Example B: I will know that I have lost weight when I can fit into my size-eight jeans.

3. Go back and rewrite the goal, using the information.

Example A: My goal is to *get promoted to the director level.*
Example B: My goal is to *fit into my size-eight jeans.*

4. Now for a little mental contrasting. Think about two positive aspects of reaching your goals and two obstacles that lie in the way.

> Example 1:
> *Positives:* I will make more money.
>   I will have more influence on the company's strategy.
> *Obstacles:* My coworker wants the same promotion.
>   I'm not sure what my boss is looking for.

5. Beginning with the first positive aspect, write a few sentences about what it will be like to experience it. Next, write a few sentences about the first obstacle, and why it's a problem. Repeat for the second positive aspect and obstacle.

How do you feel right now? If you feel as if you have a good chance of reaching your goal, you should be feeling energized and determined. *What do you need to do next?* Mental contrasting should help provide you with clarity as to your next step.

#2 Seize the Moment to Act on Your Goals

Given how busy most of us are, and how many goals we are juggling at once, it's not surprising that we routinely miss opportunities to act on a goal because we simply fail to notice them. Did you really have no time to work out today? No chance at any point to return that phone call? Achieving your goal means grabbing hold of these opportunities before they slip through your fingers.

To seize the moment, decide when and where you will take each action you want to take, in advance. Again, be as specific as possible (e.g., "If it's Monday, Wednesday, or Friday, I'll work out for thirty minutes before work"). Studies show that this kind of planning will help your brain to detect and seize the opportunity when it arises, increasing your chances of success by roughly 300 percent.

Very few of us are as productive as we could be. We *want* to be focused with laser-like precision on critical tasks and make the best, most efficient use of our time. Instead, we get distracted by coworkers, lost in our inboxes, and too absorbed by unimportant aspects of a single project, when we'd be better off turning our attention to other things.

Wanting to be more productive isn't enough to actually *make* you more productive. You need to find a way to deal effectively with the distractions, the interruptions, and the fact that there is just *way* too much on your plate. Fortunately, there is a very simple strategy that has been proven to do the trick.

It's called ***if-then*** planning, and it is a really powerful way to help you achieve any goal. Well over a hundred studies, on everything from diet and exercise to negotiation and time management, have shown that deciding in advance *when* and *where* you will take specific actions to reach your goal (e.g., "**If** it is 4 p.m., **then** I will return any phone calls I should return today") can double or triple your chances for success. Making *if-then* plans to tackle your current projects, or to reach your health or relationship goals, is probably the most effective single thing you can do to ensure your success.

If-then plans take the form:
If **X** happens, then I will do **Y**.

For example:

If I haven't written the report before lunch, **then** I will make it the first thing I do when I return.

If I am getting too distracted by colleagues, **then** I will stick to a five-minute chat limit and head back to work.

If it is 6 p.m., **then** I will spend an hour working out in the company gym before heading home.

How effective are these plans? One study looked at people who had the goal of becoming regular exercisers. Half the participants were asked to plan where and when they would exercise each week (e.g., "If it is Monday, Wednesday, or Friday, then I will hit the gym for an hour before work"). The results were dramatic: weeks later, 91 percent of *if-then* planners were still exercising regularly, compared to only 39 percent of nonplanners! Similar results have been shown for other health-promoting behaviors, like remembering to do monthly breast self-exams (100 percent of planners, 53 percent of nonplanners), and getting cervical cancer screenings (92 percent of planners, 60 percent of nonplanners).

Why are these plans so effective? Because they are written in the language of your brain—the language of *contingencies*. Human beings are particularly good at encoding and remembering information in "if X, then Y" terms, and using these contingencies to guide their behavior, often below their awareness.

Once you've formulated your *if-then* plan, your unconscious brain will start scanning the environment, searching for the situation in the "if" part of your plan. This enables you to seize the critical moment ("Oh, it's 4 p.m.! I'd better return those calls"), even when you are busy doing other things.

Since you've already decided exactly what you need to do, you can execute the plan without having to consciously think about it or waste time deliberating about what you should do next. (Sometimes this is conscious, and you actually realize you are following through on your plan. The point is it doesn't *have* to be conscious, which means your plans can get carried out when you are preoccupied with other things, and that is incredibly useful.)

So if you are finding, day after day, that too many important tasks have gone unaccomplished, and you need to introduce better habits of time management into your life by seizing opportunities to get things done, look no further: try making a simple plan. By using *if-thens* to tackle your goals, you won't *actually* be creating more hours in the day, but it will certainly feel as if you did.

Putting It into Practice: Making If-Then Plans

1. Identify a critical action you need to take to reach your goal.

2. When and where should you take this action? What is the critical situation?

3. Put it all together:
   If (or When) _____,
   then _____.

(Example: If it is 8 a.m. on Monday, then I will go for a run.)

4. Now, think about an obstacle that might derail you. This could be a temptation, a distraction, or some other factor that would interfere with your progress.

5. When that temptation or distraction comes calling, how will you handle it? What will you do instead?

6. Put it all together:
   If (or When) _____,
   then _____.
   (Example: If an e-mail from a coworker makes me angry, then I will wait thirty minutes before answering so I can respond calmly.)

#3 Know Exactly How Far You Have Left to Go

Achieving any goal also requires honest and regular monitoring of your progress—if not by others, then by you yourself. If you don't know how well you are doing, you can't adjust your behavior or your strategies accordingly. Check your progress frequently—weekly, or even daily, depending on the goal.

It's just not possible to stay motivated without feedback. No one is comfortable operating in a vacuum. Fundamentally, this is a result of the way our brains are wired. We subconsciously tune in to the presence of a *discrepancy* between where we are now and where we want to be. When your brain detects a discrepancy, it reacts by throwing resources at it: attention, effort, deeper processing of information, and willpower.

When you don't have any idea how well you're doing, or when you have only a vague sense of where you stand with respect to your goal, the discrepancy isn't clear. As a result, motivation is diminished, if not wiped out all together. It's the discrepancy that signals that an action is needed; without a discrepancy, *nothing happens*.

When you undertake a goal, you are going to need frequent feedback to maintain clarity about the progress you are (or aren't) making. If you aren't getting it from someone else, you have no choice but to seek it out yourself through self-monitoring.

Unfortunately, there is no simple rule of thumb for how often you should be assessing your progress. The optimal frequency will depend on *goal duration*. (Do you want to reach the goal this week, this year, or in five years?) For long-term goals, it makes sense to allow more time between assessments. For shorter-term goals, however, you want to assess your progress more frequently to make sure you are on track, since there is less room—or more accurately, time—for error.

Feedback frequency should also depend on where you are in the *learning curve*. Recent research suggests that you shouldn't engage in too much self-assessment when you are first trying to get the hang of something. Having to turn your attention away from what you are doing in order to process feedback is most disruptive when you are working on a task that's new and unfamiliar, creating cognitive and emotional demands that can interfere with learning and performance. So keep self-monitoring to a minimum until you have a better sense of what to do and how you should do it.

If self-monitoring and seeking out feedback are so important, you may be wondering why we don't always do it. The first and most obvious reason is that it is effortful; you need to stop whatever else you're doing and really focus on assessment. And of course, the news isn't always positive; sometimes we avoid checking in on our progress because we don't want to come face to face with how little progress we've made. (Do you ever find yourself avoiding the bathroom scale? Exactly.) So self-monitoring requires a lot of willpower (more on that later). You can make it easier by using *if-then* planning to schedule your self-assessments.

There's one more essential point to make about assessing progress. Done the right way, it will keep you motivated from start to finish. Done the wrong way, it can give you a premature sense of accomplishment that may actually lower your motivation. Recent research by University of Chicago psychologists Minjung Koo and Ayelet Fishbach examined how people pursuing goals were affected by focusing on either how far they had already come (*to-date* thinking) or what was left to be accomplished (*to-go* thinking). People routinely use both kinds of thinking when evaluating their progress. A marathon runner may choose to think about the miles already traveled or the ones that lie ahead. A dieter who wants to lose thirty pounds may try to fight temptation by reminding himself of the twenty pounds already lost, or the ten left to go.

Intuitively, both approaches have their appeal. But too much *to-date* thinking, focusing on what you've accomplished so far, will actually *undermine* your motivation to finish rather than sustain it.

Koo and Fishbach's studies consistently show that when we are pursuing a goal and consider how far we've already come, we feel a premature sense of accomplishment and begin to slack off. For instance, in one study, college students studying for an exam in an important course were significantly more motivated to study after being told that they had 52 percent of the material *left* to cover, compared to being told that they had already completed 48 percent.

When we focus on progress made, we're also more likely to try to achieve a sense of "balance" by making progress on *other* important goals. As a result, we wind up with lots of pots on the stove, but nothing is ever ready to eat.

If, instead, we focus on how far we have left to go (*to-go* thinking), motivation is not only sustained, it's heightened. So when you are assessing your progress, stay focused on the goal and never congratulate yourself too much on a job half-done. Save it for a job well—and *completely*—done.

Putting It into Practice: Monitoring Your Progress

1. Decide how often you should be assessing the progress you've made toward your goal. (This may involve some trial

and error; don't be surprised if you feel you need more or less frequent feedback down the road.)

2. Determine where the information you need to assess your progress will come from, and how you will get it. Can you completely self-assess, or do you need an objective opinion or another person's expertise?

3. Create reminders for yourself to perform your assessments. You can use your calendar, or Post-its, or create a set of *if-then* plans to assess progress at particular points. (Don't just say "I'll remember to." You're busy. You probably won't.)

4. To keep yourself motivated, always end your assessments by thinking about what

still needs to be done in order to reach
your goal—how far you have left *to go*,
rather than how far you've already come.

#4 Be a *Realistic* Optimist

When you are setting a goal, by all means engage in lots of positive thinking about how likely you are to achieve it. Believing in your ability to succeed is enormously helpful for creating and sustaining your motivation. But whatever you do, don't underestimate how difficult it will be to reach your goal. Most goals worth achieving require time, planning, effort, and persistence. Studies show that thinking things will come to you easily and effortlessly leaves you ill prepared for the journey ahead and significantly increases the odds of failure.

There are quite a number of motivational speakers and self-improvement books with a surprisingly simple message: believe that success will come easily to you, and *it will*. There is one small problem in this argument, however, which unfortunately doesn't seem to stop anyone from making it: it is utterly false.

In fact, not only is visualizing "effortless success" unhelpful, it is disastrous. This is good advice to give only if you are trying to sabotage the recipient. It is a *recipe* for failure. And no, I'm not overstating it.

But how can this be? Isn't optimism a good thing? Yes, optimism and the confidence it generates are essential for creating and sustaining the motivation you need to reach your goals. Optimists are also physically healthier, recover more quickly from illnesses, suffer less frequently from depres-

sion, are better at prioritizing and multi-
tasking, and more easily adapt to adversity
and challenges.

When you think about it, this is hardly
surprising. Albert Bandura, one of the
founding fathers of scientific psychology,
discovered decades ago that perhaps the
best predictor of individuals' success is
whether or not they *believe* they will succeed—something optimists do naturally.
Thousands and thousands of experiments
later, he has yet to be proven wrong.

But there is an important and often
overlooked caveat: to be successful, you
need to understand the very vital difference between believing you will succeed,
and believing you will succeed *easily*. Put
another way, it's the difference between being a *realistic* optimist, and an *un*realistic
optimist.

Realistic optimists (the kind Bandura was talking about) believe they will succeed, but also believe they have to *make success happen*—through things like effort, careful planning, persistence, and choosing the right strategies. They recognize the need for giving serious thought to how they will deal with obstacles. This preparation only increases their confidence in their own ability to get things done.

Unrealistic optimists, on the other hand, believe that success will *happen to them*—that the universe will reward them for all their positive thinking, or that somehow they will be transformed overnight into the kind of person for whom obstacles cease to exist. (Forgetting that even Superman had Kryptonite. And a secret identity that took a lot of trouble to maintain. And also relationship issues.)

One of the clearest illustrations of the dangers of unrealistic optimism comes from a study of weight loss. Psychologist Gabriele Oettingen asked a group of obese women who had enrolled in a weight-loss program how likely they felt they were to reach their goals. She found that those women who were confident that they would succeed lost twenty-six pounds more than self-doubters, as expected.

But Oettingen also asked the women to tell her what they imagined their road to success would be like—if they thought they would have a hard time resisting temptation, or if they'd have no problem turning down free doughnuts in the conference room and a second trip to the all-you-can-eat buffet. The results were astounding: women who believed they would succeed *easily* lost twenty-four pounds *less* than those who thought their weight-loss journey would be no walk in the park.

She has found the same pattern of results in studies of students looking for high-paying jobs after college, singles looking to find lasting love, and seniors recovering from hip replacement surgery. Realistic optimists send out more job applications, find the courage to approach potential romantic partners, and work harder on their rehabilitation exercises—in each case, leading to much higher success rates.

Believing that the road to success will be rocky leads to *greater* success, because it forces you to take action. People who are confident that they will succeed and equally confident that success won't come easily put in more effort, plan how to deal with problems before they arise, and persist longer in the face of difficulty.

Unrealistic optimists are less likely to consider all the possible turns the path to their goal might take. They are more likely to take risks without thinking things through. And they are only too happy to tell you that you are "being negative" when you dare to express concerns, harbor reservations, or dwell too long on obstacles that stand in the way of your goal. In truth, this kind of thinking is a necessary step in any successful endeavor, and it is not at all antithetical to confident optimism. Focusing *only* on what we want, to the exclusion of everything else, is just the kind of naive and reckless thinking that has landed industry leaders (and at times entire industries) in hot water.

Cultivate your realistic optimism by combining a positive attitude with an honest assessment of the challenges that await you. Don't visualize success; visualize the steps you will take in order to make success happen.

Putting It into Practice:
Be a Realistic Optimist

1. Perhaps the single most effective way to increase your confidence is to reflect on past successes. When you find yourself full of self-doubt, take a moment to recall (as vividly as possible) some of the goals you have achieved, and the obstacles you overcame to do it. You can even make this an *if-then* plan: If I am doubting myself, then I will remember the time that I _____. Studies have shown this to be an effective strategy for increasing confidence with both anxious test takers and jittery pregame athletes.

2. To keep your optimism *realistic*, think carefully about the obstacles, difficulties, and setbacks you are likely to encounter as you pursue your goal. Just as important, visualize how you will deal with each challenge. If your first strategy doesn't work, what's plan B? (This is another great time to use your *if-then* plans.) Remember, it's not "negative" to think about the problems you are likely to face, but it *is* foolish not to.

#5 Focus on *Getting Better*, Rather Than *Being Good*

Believing you have the ability to reach your goals is important, but so is believing you can *get* the ability. Many of us believe that our intelligence, our personality, and our physical aptitudes are fixed—that no matter what we do, we won't improve. As a result, we focus on goals that are all about proving ourselves, rather than developing and acquiring new skills.

Fortunately, decades of research suggest that the belief in fixed ability is completely wrong—abilities of all kinds are profoundly malleable. Embracing the fact that you can change will allow you to make better choices and reach your fullest potential. People whose goals are about getting better, rather than being good, take difficulty in stride and appreciate the journey as much as the destination.

While some may be eager to tackle a new challenge, hoping it will help them to climb the corporate ladder, many workers are really just trying to survive without committing any major screw-ups. Becoming responsible for something new and unfamiliar is understandably frightening. The odds of making a mistake increase dramatically when you are inexperienced. Small wonder that people greet a "new" assignment with so little enthusiasm.

So how can you motivate yourself to approach new responsibilities with confidence and energy? The answer is simple, though perhaps a little surprising: give yourself permission to screw up.

I know this may not be something you are thrilled to hear, because immediately you're probably thinking, "If I screw up, I'm going to be the one who pays for it." But you needn't worry about that, because studies show that when people feel they are allowed to make mistakes, they are significantly *less* likely to actually make them! Let me explain.

People approach any task with one of two types of goals: what I call *be-good* goals, where the focus is on proving that you have a lot of ability and already know what you're doing, and *get-better* goals, where the focus is on developing ability and learning to master a new skill.

The problem with *be-good* goals is that they tend to backfire when we are faced with something unfamiliar or difficult. We quickly start feeling that we don't actually know what we are doing, that we lack ability, and this creates a lot of anxiety. Countless studies have shown that *nothing* interferes with performance quite like anxiety does; it is *the* productivity killer.

Get-better goals, on the other hand, are practically bulletproof. When we think about what we are doing in terms of learning and mastering, accepting that we may make some mistakes along the way, we stay motivated despite the setbacks that might occur.

Just to give you an example, in one study I conducted a few years ago at Lehigh

University with Laura Gelety, we found that people in pursuit of *be-good* goals (i.e., trying to show how smart they already were) performed very poorly on a test of problem solving when we made the test more difficult (either by interrupting them frequently, or by throwing in a few additional unsolvable problems).

The amazing thing was that the people who were pursuing *get-better* goals (i.e., who saw the test as an opportunity to learn a new problem-solving skill) were completely *unaffected* by any of our dirty tricks. No matter how hard we made it, these participants stayed motivated and did well.

When many of us take on a new project or goal, we expect to be able to somehow do the work flawlessly, no matter how challenging it might be. Our focus is on *being good*, and the (very real) prospect of failing to meet expectations becomes terrifying. The irony is that the pressure to *be-good* results in many more mistakes, and far inferior performance, than would a focus on *getting-better*.

But that's not all. Research shows that a focus on *getting-better* also enhances the experience of working; we naturally find what we do more interesting and enjoyable when we think about it in terms of progress, rather than perfection. And lest you think that interest in your work is a mere luxury, let me assure you it is *not*; it is a powerful motivator. Finding what you do interesting and believing it has inherent value is one of the most effective ways to stay motivated despite difficulty, setbacks, and unexpected roadblocks. In fact, a recent set of studies shows that interest doesn't just keep you going despite fatigue; *it actually replenishes your energy.*

In their studies, psychologists at CSU gave participants a task to work on that was particularly draining, and then varied whether the *next* task was difficult but interesting or relatively easy but dull. They found that people who worked on the interesting task put in more effort and performed much better (despite being tired) than those who worked on the boring task, even though it was actually *harder* than the boring task. In other words, experiencing interest restored their energy and gave them a tangible advantage.

In another study, the researchers found that experiencing interest resulted in better performance on a *subsequent* task as well.

In other words, you don't just do a better job on task A because you find task A
interesting; you do a better job on follow-up
task B *because you found task A interesting*.
The replenished energy flows into whatever
you do next.

(Incidentally, each of these studies compared the effects of interest and good mood,
and found that while people do get some
replenishment of energy from happiness,
they get much more from being interested
in what they are doing. In other words, feeling engaged is the best way to keep enough
gas in your tank.)

Remember, by giving yourself permission to *not* do everything perfectly from the
start, and by acknowledging that there is a
learning curve and that improvement takes
time, you'll be taking the anxiety out of the

situation. You'll be able to better connect with what is interesting and rewarding about your work. And in so doing, you will not only increase your motivation to succeed, but also dramatically reduce the chances that you will make *any* mistakes at all.

Putting It into Practice: Focus on *Getting Better*, Rather Than *Being Good*

1. When a project is difficult and unfamiliar, remember that you will need some time to really get a handle on it. You may make some mistakes, and that's OK.

2. Use the expertise of people around you as a resource, and don't be afraid to turn to them for help when you run into trouble. People will think more of you for it, not less.

3. Don't compare yourself and your current performance to others; compare it to *your own past performance*. Are you improving? That's the question that matters. (If the answer is no, see step 2.)

#6 Have Grit

Grit is a willingness to commit to long-term goals and to persist in the face of difficulty. Studies show that gritty people obtain more education in their lifetimes and earn higher college GPAs. Grit predicts which cadets will stick out their first grueling year at West Point. In fact, grit even predicts how far contestants at the Scripps National Spelling Bee will go.

The good news is that if you aren't particularly gritty now, there is something you can do about it. People who lack grit more often than not believe that they just don't have the innate abilities successful people have. If that describes your own thinking, well, there's no way to put this nicely: you are wrong. As I mentioned earlier, effort, planning, persistence, and good strategies are what it really takes to succeed. Embracing this knowledge will not only help you see yourself and your goals more accurately, but also do wonders for your grit.

We are all impressed by demonstrations of ability. Pro athletes, computer whizzes, math geniuses, bold entrepreneurs, accomplished musicians, gifted writers—these people are widely admired because we appreciate their extraordinary aptitudes. And we envy them a little, too. You'd be hard pressed to find someone who didn't wish that he were a little smarter, a little more creative, a bit better at communicating, or perhaps more socially skilled.

Research by Stanford psychologist Carol Dweck reveals that people subscribe to one of two theories about the nature of ability. *Entity theorists* believe that their abilities are *fixed* and, more often than not, innate. They expect their performance to be relatively stable. In other words, you have just so much intelligence (or creativity, or charm), and there isn't anything you can do about it. (They are, incidentally, wrong. Ability doesn't work that way.)

Incremental theorists, on the other hand, believe that ability is *malleable*—that it can and does change with effort and experience. And according to the evidence, they are perfectly right. You can get more ability if you want more. All you need is grit.

Grit, in the sense that psychologists use the term, is persistence and commitment to long-term goals. Study after study of successful people—whether they are athletes, musicians, mathematicians, or inventors—shows that the key to success and enhanced ability is deliberate practice, thousands and thousands of hours spent mastering the necessary skills and knowledge. That kind of practice doesn't happen without grit.

Grit is all about not giving up in the face of difficulty, even when you're tired or discouraged or just plain bored. And the best predictor of not giving up is how we *explain* that difficulty in the first place. When you're having a hard time, what do you blame?

Entity theorists, who are convinced that ability is fixed, tend to blame setbacks on a *lack* of ability. *If this is hard for me, I must not be good at it.* As a result, they lack grit; they give up on themselves way too soon, inadvertently reinforcing their (mistaken) belief that they can't improve.

Incremental theorists, on the other hand, tend to blame setbacks on more control-lable factors—insufficient effort, using the wrong strategy, poor planning. When faced with difficulty, they try *harder*, armed with the belief that improvement is always possible. This gritty attitude pays off in a big way, leading to far greater long-term accomplishments.

Interestingly, recent research suggests that entity theorists not only lack the grit needed to improve, but actually find improvement to be, often unconsciously, anxiety provoking because they believe it shouldn't be *possible.*

In studies conducted by University of Toronto psychologists Jason Plaks and Kristin Stecher, college students were given difficult reasoning problems. After the first round, everyone received feedback that he or she performed at the sixty-first percentile. Next, all of the students were given a lesson on how to approach solving the problems, including tips and strategies. After a second round of problems, some students were told that their performance had not changed, while others were told that it had improved to the ninety-first percentile.

Not surprisingly, everyone who improved was happy to have done so, but entity theorists, believing that they really *shouldn't* have improved, also reported significant increases in *anxiety*. The more anxiety they felt, the worse they performed on a third set of problems that followed. (In fact, entity theorists who were told that they *didn't* improve did better on the third set than those who were told that they did!)

So when we don't *expect* to improve, does this mean we actually prefer *not* to improve? I wouldn't go that far. Everyone welcomes improvement, but only for entity theorists does that improvement come with anxiety. That anxiety, in turn, undermines future performance, eroding our confidence that improvement was ever actually real.

Looking back, these studies have given me some insight into some episodes in my own life. For instance, take my experience with billiards. I freely admit that I am a *terrible* pool player. I played a few times in college and it was a sorry sight. I wrote the game off quickly, believing that I just didn't have the hand-eye coordination to ever be any good at it. (I should mention that I had a long track record of lacking hand-eye coordination. When my brother tried to teach me to catch a ball in our backyard when I was ten, I caught it with my face and broke my nose.)

Years ago I dated an avid pool player, who convinced me one night at our neighborhood bar to give the game another chance. Before beginning, he gave me a brief lesson—how to hold the cue, how to line up a shot, and so on. We played, and something totally unexpected happened—I played *well*. In fact, I came awfully close to beating him. And I remember feeling both elated that I had improved, and completely freaked out. Did I *really* improve? How was that possible? *I'm not good at this sort of thing.* Maybe it was a fluke.

A few days later we played again, and I approached the table with a nervousness I hadn't felt before, even when I thought I'd play terribly. What would happen? I had no idea. And that nervousness wreaked havoc on my ability to play. I couldn't sink a ball to save my life. *I knew it was a fluke*, I thought. *I'm definitely not good at this sort of thing.*

Granted, we're talking about playing pool here, and I realize that it's not a skill that usually has life-altering consequences. But what if it was? What if instead of writing off my pool-playing ability, I had written off my ability to do math, learn to use complex computer programs, write well, take on leadership roles, be creative, embrace risk, give compelling presentations, or become more socially skilled? What if I believed that I couldn't improve when it came to something that *really mattered*?

The bottom line is, no matter what kind of learning opportunities you are given, you probably aren't going to see lasting improvement if, deep down, you don't believe improvement is possible. You just won't have the grit for it. If improvement isn't possible, it makes no sense to try, especially when the going is tough. Believing that your ability is fixed becomes a self-fulfilling prophecy, and the self-doubt it creates will sabotage you in the end.

To be successful and truly make the most of your potential, **it's critical to *examine* your beliefs, and when necessary, *challenge them*.** Change really *is* always possible, and the science here is crystal clear. There is *no* ability that can't be developed with experience. The next time you find yourself thinking, "But I'm just not good at this," remember: you're just not good at it *yet*.

Putting It into Practice: Get Grit

1. Are there aspects of your job that you
   feel you aren't good at? Take a moment
   to think about that. Be honest.

2. Now, deep down, do you believe you can
   become good at them, or do you think
   you are stuck just as you are? If it's the
   latter, your belief has been doing you
   a great injustice, because it's wrong.
   Remember that improvement is *always*
   possible.

3. Challenge that entity thinking whenever
   you catch yourself succumbing to it!
   When you focus on improving and developing your skills, you naturally become
   grittier in pursuit of your goals.

#7 Build Your Willpower Muscle

Your self-control "muscle" is just like the other muscles in your body; when it doesn't get much exercise, it becomes weaker over time. But when you give it regular work-outs by putting it to good use, it will grow stronger and stronger, and better able to help you successfully reach your goals.

To build willpower, take on a challenge that requires you to do something you'd honestly rather not do. Give up high-fat snacks, do a hundred sit-ups a day, stand up straight when you catch yourself slouching, try to learn a new skill. When you find yourself wanting to give in, give up, or just not bother—don't. Start with just one activity and make a plan for how you will deal with troubles when they occur ("If I have a craving for a snack, I will eat one piece of fresh or three pieces of dried fruit"). It will be hard in the beginning, but it will get easier, and that's the whole point. As your strength grows, you can take on more challenges and step up your self-control workout.

Many of the goals we struggle with year after year have one thing in common: *resisting temptation*. Trying to ignore the powerful allure of the forbidden cigarette, doughnut, or latest budget-blowing buying impulse requires willpower. When faced with a boring expense report or a dense white paper, it takes self-control to avoid checking Facebook, answering e-mail, or firing up a game of solitaire. And for some, it takes even more strength of will to keep their temper in check at work when a colleague "just doesn't get it" or a subordinate makes a mistake.

You might expect very successful people, who presumably have boatloads of willpower, to be particularly good at not giving in. But if anything, they seem to be *even more* susceptible to temptation than the rest of us. Quick—name a famous or powerful person who doesn't have a well-known weakness for something. I'll wait.

Having the willpower to govern a country, yet lacking the willpower to resist cigarettes or french fries may seem like a contradiction, but it actually isn't, according to research on the nature of self-control.

To understand why, you need to understand how willpower really works.

Your capacity for self-control is not unlike the muscles in your body. Like biceps or triceps, willpower can vary in its strength, not only from person to person, but *from moment to moment*. Just as well-developed biceps sometimes get tired and jellylike after a strenuous workout, so too does your willpower "muscle."

Even everyday actions like decision making or trying to make a good impression can sap this valuable resource, as can coping with the stresses of your career and family. When you tax it too much at once, or for too long, the well of self-control runs dry. It is in these moments that the doughnut wins.

The good news is that willpower depletion is only temporary. Give your muscle time to bounce back, and you'll be back in fighting form and ready to say no to any doughnuts that come your way. Recent research shows that when rest is not an option, you can actually speed up your self-control recovery or give it a boost when reserves are low, simply by *thinking* about people you know who have a lot of self-control. (Thinking about my impossibly self-possessed mother does wonders for me when I'm tempted to snap at someone.)

Or, you can try giving yourself a pick-me-up. I don't mean a cocktail; I mean something that puts you in a good mood. (Again, *not* a cocktail—it may be mood enhancing, but alcohol is definitely not will-power enhancing.) Anything that lifts your spirits—listening to a favorite song, watching a funny video, calling a good friend, or reflecting on a past success—should also help restore your self-control strength when you're looking for a quick fix.

The other way in which willpower is like a muscle (and the really *great* news for those of us struggling to get our impulses under control) is that it can be made stronger over time, if you give it regular workouts. Recent studies show that daily activities such as exercising, keeping track of your finances or what you are eating—or even just remembering to sit up straight every time you think of it—can strengthen your capacity for self-control. For example, in one study, people who were given free gym memberships and stuck to a daily exercise program for two months not only got physically healthier, but also smoked fewer cigarettes, drank less alcohol, and ate less junk food. They were better able to control their tempers and less likely to spend money impulsively. They didn't leave their dishes in the sink, didn't put things off until later, and missed fewer appointments. In fact, every aspect of their lives that required the use of willpower improved dramatically.

So if you want to build more willpower, start by picking an activity (or avoiding one) that fits with your life and your goals—anything that requires you to override an impulse or desire again and again—and add this activity to your daily routine. Examples from past research include giving up a favorite sweet, refraining from cursing, using your nondominant hand to open doors and brush your teeth, and avoiding starting sentences with "I." But you can choose just about anything for your self-control exercise, so long as it involves overcoming an urge—doing something you'd rather not do. Depending on your habits, making your bed each morning or limiting your time on Facebook might be a good place to start. It will be hard in the beginning, but it will get easier over time if you hang in there, because your capacity for self-control will grow.

Putting It into Practice: Pump Up Your Self-Control Muscle

1. Willpower gets depleted with use. When the tank is empty, give yourself a rest before tackling a new self-control challenge.

2. You can speed up your recovery by doing something to lift your spirits, reward-

ing yourself for good behavior, or by just thinking about someone you know with lots of self-control.

3. Your willpower muscle will grow with regular exercise. Before taking on a goal that requires *lots* of willpower (e.g., quitting smoking, radically changing your diet), start by strengthening your muscle with regular, less strenuous workouts. Add a few willpower challenges to your day (e.g., making your bed, sitting up straight, taking the stairs instead of the elevator) and build from there.

#8 Don't Tempt Fate

No matter how strong your willpower muscle becomes, it's important to always respect the fact that it is limited, and if you overtax it, you will temporarily run out of steam. Don't try to take on two challenging goals at once, if you can help it (like quitting smoking and dieting at the same time). And make achieving your goal easier by keeping yourself out of harm's way. Many people are overly confident in their ability to resist temptation, and as a result they put themselves in situations where temptations abound. Successful people know not to make reaching a goal harder than it already is.

Resisting temptation is a key part of successfully reaching just about any goal. What we *want* to do is often the very opposite of what we *need* to do in order to achieve our professional or personal ambitions. This may sound a bit counterintuitive, but the very first thing you are going to want to do if you are serious about resisting temptation—even before you start working on building your willpower muscle—is make peace with the fact that your willpower is limited. It will *always* be limited, even if you get more of it through regular exercise. (Remember that no matter how big a muscle is, it can still be overworked.)

The problem is that most of us think we have more willpower than we actually do. As a result, we put ourselves in harm's way, exposing ourselves to temptations that we assume we'll be able to handle. For example, in one study of smoking cessation, participants who hadn't smoked in three weeks (and were therefore well out of the physical withdrawal phase) were asked how confident they felt about resisting the desire to smoke in the future. They were also asked about whether or not they planned to avoid temptation—the situations (like being out with friends who smoke) that might increase their urge to smoke. The results showed that the more confident the former smokers were about their ability to resist temptation, the more likely they were to tempt fate. Several months later, smokers who *did* avoid temptation were less likely to have relapsed, while those who overestimated their willpower returned to their old habits.

Even if you have built up large reserves of willpower, you will not have much left for sticking to your resolutions at the end of a long day of putting out fires at work. (This is basically why Happy Hour exists.) Don't kid yourself; during particularly stressful times, you will have a hard time staying on track. That's why it's so important to give some thought to when you are most likely to feel drained and vulnerable, and *make an if-then plan* to keep yourself out of harm's way. Be prepared with an alternate activity, a distraction, or a low-calorie snack, which-ever applies.

Also, do yourself a favor, and don't try to pursue two goals at once that each requires a lot of self-control, if you can help it. This is really just asking for trouble. For ex-ample, studies show that people who try to quit smoking *while* dieting, in order to avoid the temporary weight gain that often accompanies smoking cessation, are more likely to fail at *both* enterprises than people who tackle them one at a time.

Finally, remember that it is far easier to abstain from doing something all together than it is to give in just a little and *then* stop. And you need more and more self-control to stop a behavior the longer it goes on. If you don't want to end up having sex, it's best to stop at the goodnight kiss. If you're trying to lose weight, it's best to pass up the potato chip bowl altogether. Remember the slogan, "Betcha can't eat just one." Lay's wasn't kidding.

Putting It into Practice:
Stop Before You Start

1. If you have a bad habit you're trying to kick or an impulse you are trying to

resist, give some thought to the times and situations in which you are most vulnerable to temptation and how you can avoid them if possible.

2. Tackle major willpower challenges one at a time. (If people stuck to just one New Year's resolution per year, they would be a lot more successful.)

3. Avoid thinking you can have "just one" or "a little bit" of something you *really* enjoy but shouldn't have. It is easier to skip it entirely. Less fun, but much easier.

#9 Focus on What You *Will* Do, Not What You *Won't* Do

Do you want to successfully get promoted, quit smoking, or put a lid on your bad temper? Then plan how you will replace counterproductive behaviors with more constructive, profitable ones. Too often, people concentrate all their efforts on what they want to *stop* doing and fail to consider how they will fill the void. Research on thought suppression (e.g., "Don't think about white bears!") has shown that trying to avoid a thought makes it even more active in your mind. The same holds true when it comes to behavior; by trying *not* to do something, the impulse gets strengthened rather than diminished.

If you want to change your ways, ask yourself, what will I do instead? For example, if you are trying to gain control of your temper and stop flying off the handle, you might make a plan such as, "If I am starting to feel angry, then I will take three deep breaths to calm down." By using deep breathing as a replacement for giving in to your anger, your success-sabotaging impulse will get worn away over time until it disappears completely.

Once you've decided to make an *if-then* plan to help you reach your goal, the next thing you need to do is figure out what *exactly* goes in it. According to new research, you need to be very careful about the way you word your plan, because one particular type of *if-then* plan can backfire, leaving you doing *more* of whatever you were trying to avoid doing in the first place.

Researchers from Utrecht University in the Netherlands looked at three types of *if-then* plans. **Replacement** plans do just what the name suggests—replace a negative behavior with a more positive one. If you have a tendency to immediately say yes to every opportunity that comes your way, and you end up with *way* too many pots on the stove, you might create an *if-then* replacement plan such as, "If I am offered a new project, then I will think it over for at least twenty-four hours before responding." "Think it over for twenty-four hours" is a replacement behavior—a more adaptive response designed to substitute for whatever you usually do that gets you into trouble.

Ignore if-then plans are focused on blocking out unwanted feelings, like cravings, performance anxiety, or self-doubts. ("If I have the urge to smoke, then I will ignore it.") In this case, you are simply planning to tune out unwanted impulses and thoughts in order to diminish their effect on you.

Finally, **negation** *if-then* plans involve spelling out the actions you *won't* be taking in the future. With these plans, if there is a behavior you want to avoid, you simply plan *not* to perform this behavior. ("If I am at the mall, then I won't buy anything.") This is, in a sense, the most straightforward and head-on way of addressing negative impulses, and probably the one we most often end up using.

All three types of *if-then* plans were put to the test, with surprising and consistent results. The researchers found that **negation** *if-then* plans not only were far less effective compared to other plans, but sometimes resulted in a *rebound* effect, leading people to do more of the forbidden behavior than before.

Just as research on thought suppression (e.g., "Don't think about white bears!") has shown that constantly monitoring for a thought makes it more active in your mind, negation *if-then* plans keep the focus on the suppressed behavior. Ironically, by simply planning *not* to engage in impulsive actions, the impulse gets *strengthened* rather than broken. So a plan such as, "If I go to the mall, then I won't buy anything," may end up costing you a small fortune.

Remember that when it comes to reaching your goals, you need to plan how you will replace the behaviors that sabotage your success with better ones, rather than focusing only on the maladaptive behaviors themselves. The critical part of your *if-then* plan is what you *will* do, not what you won't do.

Putting It into Practice: Focus on What You *Will* Do

1. Many of our goals have to do with stopping something: *not* overeating, *not* overworking, *not* staying up so late, *not* being so defensive. But thinking about a goal in this way can actually strengthen our self-sabotaging impulses, rather than wear them down. Reframe a *stopping*

goal in terms of starting: decide what you will do *instead*.

2. Once you've decided on the good be-havior that will replace the undesirable one, make an *if-then* plan: If I feel the urge to _____, then I will _____ instead.

Conclusion

Most of us look at people at the top of their game—the captains of industry, the wielders of political power, the movers and shakers in the arts, film, and music—and explain their successes using words like "genius," "ability," and "talent." Which would be fine if most of us understood how genius, ability, and talent *work.* Being successful is *not* about winning the DNA lottery; it's about reaching goals. It's about making smart choices, using the right strategies, and taking action. Study after study shows that so-called "innate" ability measures, like

IQ, do a remarkably poor job predicting who succeeds and who doesn't. Measures of effective strategy use and persistence, on the other hand, tell us *a lot* about who is likely to rise to the top.

Successful people set very specific goals and seize opportunities to act on them (using strategies like *if-then* planning). They always know how far they have to go and stay focused on what still needs to be done. They believe they will succeed, but embrace the fact that success will not come easily. They remember that it's about making progress, rather than doing everything perfectly right out of the gate. They believe that they can develop their abilities through effort, which makes them gritty in the face of setbacks and challenges. They build their willpower through frequent exercise, make plans for how to cope when willpower is low, and try not to put themselves in situations where temptations abound. They focus on what they *will* do, rather than what they won't do.

There is nothing they do that *you* can't do, too.

For more scientifically proven strategies you can use to achieve personal and professional success, check out my new book *Succeed: How We Can Reach Our Goals*.

Notes

Introduction

p. 2 **These are the nine things that successful people do—the strategies they use to set and pursue goals (sometimes without consciously realizing it) that, according to decades of research...** Gordon B. Moskowitz and Heidi Grant, eds, *The Psychology of Goals* (New York: The Guildford Press, 2009).

Chapter 1

p. 7 **Thousands of studies have shown that getting specific...** Edwin A. Locke and Gary P. Latham, "Building a Practically Useful Theory of Goal Setting and Task Motivation: A 35-Year Odyssey," American Psychologist 57, no. 9 (2002): 705–717.

p. 9 **In studies my colleagues and I have conducted...** Angela Lee Duckworth, Heidi Grant, Benjamin Loew, Gabriele Oettingen, and Peter M. Gollwitzer, "Self-Regulation Strategies Improve Self-Discipline in Adolescents: Benefits of Mental Contrasting and Implementation Intentions," *Educational Psychology: An International Journal of Experimental Educational Psychology* 31, no. 1 (2011): 17–26.

Chapter 2

p. 17 **Well over a hundred studies, on everything from diet and exercise...**

Peter M. Gollwitzer and Paschal Sheeran, "Implementation Intentions and Goal Achievement: A Meta-Analysis of Effects and Processes," *Advances in Experimental Psychology*, 38 (2006): 69–119.

p. 18 **One study looked at people who had the goal of becoming regular exercisers.** Sarah Milne, Sheina Orbell, and Paschal Sheeran, "Combining Motivational and Volitional Interventions to Promote Exercise Participation: Protection Motivation Theory and Implementation Intentions," *British Journal of Health Psychology* 7, no. 2 (May 2002): 163–184.

Chapter 3

p. 25 **Recent research suggests that you shouldn't engage in too much self-as-**

sessment... Chak Fu Lam, D. Scott DeRue, Elizabeth P. Karam, and John R. Hollenbeck, "The Impact of Feedback Frequency on Learning and Task Performance: Challenging the 'More is Better' Assumption," *Organizational Behavior and Human Decision Processes* 116, no. 2 (November 2011): 217–228.

p. 27 **Recent research by University of Chicago psychologists...** Minjung Koo and Ayelet Fishbach, "Dynamics of Self-Regulation: How (Un)accomplished Goal Actions Affect Motivation," *Journal of Personality and Social Psychology* 94, no. 2 (February 2008): 183–195.

Chapter 4

p. 37 **One of the clearest illustrations of the dangers of unrealistic optimism...** Gabriele Oettingen and Thomas A. Wadden, "Expectation, Fantasy, and Weight Loss: Is the Impact of Positive Thinking Always Positive?" *Cognitive Therapy and Research* 15, no. 2 (1991): 167–175.

p. 38 **She has found the same pattern of results in studies of students...** Gabriele Oettingen and Doris Mayer, "The Motivating Function of Thinking about the Future: Expectations versus Fantasies," *Journal of Personality and Social Psychology* 83, no. 5 (November 2002): 1198–1212.

p. 40 **Studies have shown this to be an effective strategy for increasing confidence...** Anja Achtziger, Peter M. Gollwitzer, and Paschal Sheeran, "Implementation Intentions and Shielding Goal Striving From Unwanted Thoughts and Feelings,"

Personality and Social Psychology Bulletin 34, no. 3 (March 2008): 381–393.

Chapter 5

p. 46 **Just to give you an example, in one study I conducted...** Gordon B. Moskowitz and Heidi Grant, eds, *The Psychology of Goals* (New York: The Guildford Press, 2009).

p. 48 **In fact, a recent set of studies shows that interest...** Dustin B. Thoman, Jessi L. Smith, and Paul J. Silvia, "The Resource Replenishment Function of Interest," *Social Psychological and Personality Science* 2, no. 6 (November 2011): 592–599.

Chapter 6

p. 55 **Research by Stanford psychologist Carol Dweck...** Carol S. Dweck, *Mindset:*

The New Psychology of Success (New York: Ballantine Books, 2008).

Chapter 7

p. 69 **Recent research shows that when rest is not an option...** Michelle R. vanDellen and Rick H. Hoyle, "Regulatory Accessibility and Social Influences on State Self-Control," *Personality and Social Psychology Bulletin* 36, no. 2 (February 2010): 251–263.

p. 70 **For example, in one study, people who were given free gym memberships...** Megan Oaten and Ken Chang, "Longitudinal Gains in Self-Regulation from Regular Physical Exercise," *British Journal of Health Psychology* 11, no. 4 (November 2006): 717–733.

p. 71 **Examples from past research include giving up a favorite sweet...** Roy F.

Baumeister, Matthew Gailliot, C. Nathan DeWall, and Megan Oaten, "Self-Regulation and Personality: How Interventions Increase Regulatory Success, and How Depletion Moderates the Effects of Traits on Behavior," *Journal of Personality* 74, no. 6 (December 2006): 1773–1802.

Chapter 8

p. 77 **For example, in one study of smoking cessation...** Loran F. Nordgren, Frenk van Harreveld, and Joop van der Pligt, "The Restraint Bias: How the Illusion of Self-Restraint Promotes Impulsive Behavior," *Psychological Science* 20, no. 12 (December 2009): 1523–1528.

Chapter 9

p. 82 **According to new research, you need to be very careful about the way you**

word your plan… Marieke A. Adriaanse, Johanna M. F. van Oosten, Denise T. D. de Ridder, John B. F. de Wit, and Catharine Evers, "Planning What Not to Eat: Ironic Effects of Implementation Intentions Negating Unhealthy Habits," *Personality and Social Psychology Bulletin* 37, no. 1 (January 2011): 69–81.

Conclusion

p. 89 **Study after study shows that so-called "innate" ability measures…** Angela L. Duckworth and Martin E. P. Seligman, "Self-Discipline Outdoes IQ in Predicting Academic Performance of Adolescents," *Psychological Science* 16, no. 12 (December 2005): 939–944.

Acknowledgments

I am so grateful to the superb team at Harvard Business Publishing—especially to Tim Sullivan, who believed my "Nine Things" post might just make a good e-single, and Sarah Green, who helped me to actually make it one. Many thanks also to Whitney Johnson, who opened the door for me at *Harvard Business Review*, and to my agent and friend Giles Anderson, who helped open that one, and so many more.

About the Author

Heidi Grant Halvorson, PhD, is a social psychologist, speaker, and author of *Succeed: How We Can Reach Our Goals* (Hudson Street Press, 2011). She is also Associate Director of Columbia Business School's Motivation Science Center, serves on the advisory boards of several companies, and is an expert blogger on motivation and leadership for *Harvard Business Review, Huffington Post, Forbes, Fast Company,* and *Psychology Today.* Her original post "Nine Things Successful People Do Differently" holds the

HBR record for most unique views in the history of the Web site. Grant Halvorson offers corporate training on the subjects of motivation, persuasion, and marketing. Follow her on Twitter @hghalvorson or at *www.heidigranthalvorson.com.*